FINDING THE

VOICE

OF THE

SOUL

∞

A Bold Path Inviting

Consciousness and Compassion

FINDING THE VOICE OF THE SOUL

∞

A Bold Path Inviting

Consciousness and Compassion

JOSEPH M. BERNARD, PH.D.

ISBN: 978-0-9887703-4-8

Wild Ginger Press
www.wildgingerpress.com

*For all who expand their minds and open their hearts
on the path of compassion, consciousness and freedom.*

ACKNOWLEDGMENT

I want to acknowledge the people who have helped this book come into form.

First, my wife Bobbi Benson. She is a wonderful book designer and she graciously agreed to design this book. I am deeply grateful for her skills, her patience and her efforts.

Second, I want to thank my niece, Erin Bernard, for her valuable editing and helpful recommendations. She is also an amazing writer.

And third, I appreciate the voice of my soul that has inspired this entire book and keeps inspiring me every day of my life.

∞

CONTENTS

∞

INTRODUCTION

A round the 10th anniversary of the 9/11 attacks, I had been thinking about how it was time for our country to change course and move away from war and toward a more peaceful way of being in the world. I wondered: What it would take to redirect this nation and in fact, all nations, toward the realization of the many commonalities humans share instead of the ideological conflicts that have dominated human history?

There seems to be much more hope in exploring the common ground we share instead of battling until the last person is standing. The finding and exploration of common ground would represent the expansion of consciousness of all humanity; the battling till the last person is standing represents the very old model that has been dominating the world for centuries.

As I look out into the world I see reasons to be hopeful. Many of you are seeking ways to expand your consciousness and encourage the evolutionary process for the benefit of all life on the planet. There is a real possibility that together you and I can reach higher levels of compassion and consciousness in the ways each of us interacts with others. Both together and individually we are rich in possibilities and potential that can blossom into powerful forces for positive change.

Here's how I see the world now: There are two inner voices that direct what is possible for your life, and for all of humanity. These two voices are very different in outlook and in the way they affect all of us.

The noisiest and more dominant of

those two voices is the

VOICE OF THE EGO-MIND

and the quieter and wiser one is the

VOICE OF THE SOUL.

The simple definition of those two voices is that the *Voice Of the Ego* (**VOE**) is the voice in your head that is about protecting you from all the fears you think you have. This VOE is past- and future-focused, so it obsesses about how it can repair what happened in the past and take control of what happens in the future. This voice is not bad; it is driven by the survival urge in you. You could say this is the voice of the biological imperative for survival. It is a powerful and necessary voice.

INFINITE
MIND

VOICE OF THE
SOUL
(HIGHER MIND)

VOICE OF
THE EGO
(ORDINARY
MIND)

Ego does not exist as far as a place in the body or mind but seems to inform you about certain aspects of how you should function. Don't for a second underestimate this voice's power within you. The ego-mind is the source of all fear, all anger, all hate, all war, all need to dominate, all win/lose thinking, all "I am right, you are wrong" opinions, and the basis from which the political process is formulated and the religious hierarchy has been established. Again, this is not a "bad" force. It is about survival driven by fear.

The *Voice Of the Soul* (VOS) is the voice of your higher nature. This voice resides in the present and is calming, peaceful, loving and hopeful. The voice of your soul can be understood as the voice of your higher mind, your infinite spirit and/or your intuition. This voice represents what is possible for you when you are free of fear and open in mind and heart. You can call this the voice of what is eternal and infinite within you—your expression of the Source of all creation.

You could insert any of these four different "S" words to accurately describe the voice of your highest possibilities: Spirit, Soul, Self (Higher) and Sanity. They all mean about the same thing but each represents something different energetically. "Sanity" is about heeding a sane voice inside of you instead of listening to the insanity of the ego, which is run by fear and able to rationalize anything. The "Self" that is higher than the "self" of the ego makes sense also because it is not caught up in fear and the need to be in control. "Soul" works

OTHER NAMES FOR VOS AND VOE

Higher Self — **VOICE OF THE SOUL** LIVING IN THE NOW — Expanded Mind
Wise Mind — Spirit
Pure Awareness — Higher Consciousness
Compassionate Heart — Self

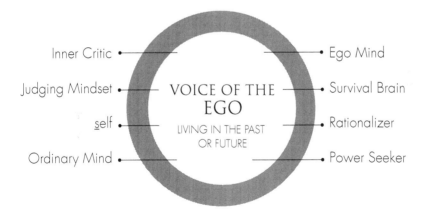

Inner Critic — **VOICE OF THE EGO** LIVING IN THE PAST OR FUTURE — Ego Mind
Judging Mindset — Survival Brain
self — Rationalizer
Ordinary Mind — Power Seeker

well and I chose it because it represents a part of you that existed before this lifetime and will exist after this body dies. "Spirit" seems similar to soul but is more like the energy of the divine that is within you. Soul works the best from my viewpoint. You can safely substitute any of these words. As you read this book, I invite you to use whatever "S" words work for you.

The Soul, like the ego, is not a physical reality but also represents a powerful force within. The soul is the voice calling you to learn and grow, to seek your higher expression, to love and be compassionate, to explore what is possible in you, to have purpose and to make a positive difference. Your intuition is often the direct line to your soul. This is the force for transformation, for higher consciousness and for the highest realization of you as a human being. The voice of the soul invites you into the silence to hear and be guided to your fullest expression.

A Personal Note For You

I hope the ideas I write about in this book will inspire you or point you in a direction that is right for you. You, of course, must find your own way to what is true, but having help can encourage new perspectives and invite new insights. My hope is that with fresh ideas you can find what truly matters most to you and gain clarity about your own truth.

Why this book? In my heart I am both a spiritual seeker and a social activist. I am both an inward traveler and a compassionate social change-agent. These two inner drives often seem to draw me in different directions. The inner part wants to be quiet and the activist wants to shout, "What the hell is going on?" (Maybe you can identify with the inner drive of different aspects of yourself?) After much searching as to how I might integrate these two aspects of myself, I decided to start writing about both the wisdom of the inner journey and the importance of being engaged in the world in constructive ways.

My blog (ExploreLifeBlog.com) was the starting point of this writing and still flows with much inspiration. Now I want to put together the best ideas and wisdom I have gathered together from my inner questioning, my readings, my work with clients and my passion for positive change. This book is an outgrowth of that desire to be a seeker and a change agent.

There are many people out there like me who also want to speak up and not lose their center. The bookshelves reflect the movement toward integrating the highest human wisdom and birthing real social change. This book is unique because it is my take on how to merge this integration of engagement while still remaining peaceful inside, and looking at the interior landscape of the voices that influence how you and I are in the world.

The times are ripe for change. You and I are now present on the planet at this very rich time when there is great potential for positive change. Maybe, just maybe, you are here to make things happen. I trust that if you are reading this you also feel the draw toward something greater within you.

If you take the time to look inward as you travel through this book, you can become a
FOCUSED AND DYNAMIC POSITIVE FORCE IN THE WORLD.

You have a richness of possibilities. I want to assist you in any way I can to make the most out of your life.

Joseph Bernard
Summer 2013

CHAPTER ONE

The Experience Of Two Powerful Voices

As I began writing this book I was clear about the importance of the message but struggled with how I would write about the ideas in a way that would be lucid and useful. I decided to write directly from my heart, and from the highest knowing I was able to share with you at this time in my own exploration of truth. Like you, I am imperfect, but that does not hold me back from presenting inspired ideas that I am confident will enrich your life and act as a positive force for a better world.

First I want to further share the characteristics of these two voices in the human experience. As you become acquainted with them, you can take this information and expand your awareness of which voice is guiding you in different aspects of your life. The powerful thing about awareness is that as you understand who you are, you can build on the aspects that you value and that are working for you, and you can choose to change the aspects that are limiting for you. Awareness equals choice and with choice change is clearly possible.

AWARENESS = CHOICE = CHANGE

Characteristics Of
The *Voice Of The Soul* (VOS)

There are definite characteristics of what I am describing as the *Voice of the Soul*. Here is my list of characteristics. To make this more meaningful, keep track of which characteristics describe you:

+ Led by the heart
_____

+ Guided by compassion
_____

+ Quiet wisdom
_____

+ Humility
_____

+ Genuineness
_____

+ Intuitive
_____

+ Calm
_____

+ Peaceful
_____

+ Impartial, non-judging

+ Kind self witness

+ Open-minded

+ Inclusive

+ Accepting

+ Appreciative

+ Centered

+ Mindful

+ Listens with kindness

+ Seeks to understand

+ Self-realized

+ Seeks truth

+ In touch with inner knowing

+ One with Higher Self

+ Compassionate observer of the dramas of life

+ Cares for self and others

+ Confident

+ Appreciates diversity

+ Questions your thoughts

+ Relaxed

+ Lives in the now—is present

+ Happy

+ Focused with clear intention

+ Learns from all points of view

+ Acknowledging and accepting of all emotions

+ Positive

+ Hopeful

+ Takes responsibility

+ Trusts self and trusts the universe

+ Seeks insights, awareness and understanding

+ Values silence

+ Interested in higher consciousness and personal growth

+ Able to find peace of mind

+ Aligned with Unity Consciousness

+ Lives according to your own values

+ Respectful of self and others

+ Treats the body with respect

+ Acts with kindness

+ Seeks personal freedom

+ Inwardly aware

+ Respects inner desires

+ Purposeful with passion

+ Seeks the light

+ Comfortable with self

+ Able to play and have fun

I am sure there are other positive characteristics. How many did you note as describing you? What would you add to this list? If you noted many of these characteristics, then you are a person who has begun to awaken to what is possible within. You're awakening to your light, to what is possible in you, is a genuine gift to those around you and to the rest of us on the planet.

Characteristics Of The *Voice Of The Ego* (VOE)

These characteristics of the *Voice of the Ego* are best thought of as areas in need of improvement rather than flaws to be judged harshly. I would encourage you to note which ones describe you—*but that might be a mistake from what I understand about human nature.* That understanding would suggest you may note which ones fit for you as a way of criticizing who you are. For most of us, it is easier to note our faults than to note what we appreciate about ourselves. My understanding of the characteristics of the ego-mind's voice include the following:

✦   Needs to be in charge

✦   Is sure it's right

✦   Lives in fear

✦   Feels desperate about the world

✦   Wants to control situations and other people

✦   Obsessed with the past

✦   Worried about the future

- Run by the chaos of the mind

- Angry

- Blaming and complaining

- Not able to trust

- Full of self-doubt

- Closed-minded

- Blocked and/or protected heart

- Run by unquestioned beliefs

- Uptight

- In a hurry

- Negative

- Hateful

- Boastful

- Noisy

- Has to be heard

- Seeks attention

+ Not insight-oriented

+ Highly competitive

+ Hates to lose at anything

+ Believes their own thoughts

+ Over confident in actions

+ Much self-doubt underneath

+ Uncomfortable with silence

+ Unable to quiet the mind

+ Difficulty with relationships

+ Not interested in listening to different perspectives or points of view

+ Able to rationalize all kinds of irrational behavior

+ Run by habits and addictions

+ Claims to be moral but lives in conflict with stated values

+ Low tolerance for others

+ Argues for freedom but traps self with limiting thoughts

+ Out of touch with self, thoughts and emotions

+ Distrustful of innate desires

+ Worries about the approval of others

+ Run by their own darkness

+ Doesn't like to be seen, uncomfortable with self

+ Seeks attention

+ Separate

+ Contracted and closed down

+ Too serious, can't have fun

+ Unhappy and depressed

+ Resistant

+ Full of worry and hurry

+ Suffers because of his or her own thoughts

+ Self-destructive

+ Isolated in the heart

There are most likely additional indicators of the ego being in charge but this is more than enough. If you identify with a number of these qualities, then you are like most humans. To be human is to have an ego that wants to protect you by running your life. Did you more easily note what is not okay about you?

This easy-to-judge self is part of the way

the ego-mind keeps its power.

The more you feel bad about yourself

THE MORE YOU LET
THE EGO BE IN CHARGE.

The *Voice of the Soul* and the *Voice of the Ego* have significant influence over your life. The VOE is usually the dominating force. The VOS too often plays a minor role unless you make a point of growing that voice inside of you. If the VOE is in charge, your life is full of fear, anger, mistrust and unrest. This ego voice wants you to be safe so it does all it can to make you hyper-tuned into all that could go wrong. This focus on what might go wrong jams your inner airways and keeps you uptight and unable to be present to your deeper knowing.

There are real dangers in letting yourself actually believe the rants of the ego. This makes for a very uneasy existence unless you numb out through distractions such as television, computer games, entertainment, living in the world of blaming and complaining, getting caught up in other people's dramas, abusing substances like alcohol or drugs, or simply denying how you are feeling and living in despair. (This may sound dreary, but as a therapist, I have seen many people do everything they can to numb out to life).

On a much lighter note, let's look at what the VOS can bring to your life. This voice is who you are beyond the made-up story of the ego-mind. You have no reason to numb out if you live under the guidance of your soul. Life is full of possibilities if you are soul guided. You can be much more than the dramas you get caught up in. You can have purpose, be compassionate, be creative, be full of life, be highly conscious and aware and be inspired and uplifted.

The *Voice of the Soul* has great hope for you and what you are capable of becoming. Your soul realizes that you have much to offer through the unique expression of who you are. When you listen inwardly, the VOS will always be there to guide you toward what is possible in the now of your life.

Let's talk about the benefits of following the wise voice of your soul. These benefits include:

✦ You feel at peace inside

✦ You tune in intuitively

+ There is a sense of synchronicity in how things unfold

+ Your creativity is alive and well

+ You have trust in yourself and in the process

+ The right things seem to fall into place

+ Doors open

+ Energy increases

+ Your heart is engaged

+ You mind is relaxed and ready

+ You feel connected to the world around you

+ Opportunities arise effortlessly

+ You feel alive and energized

+ There is much inspiration available to you

+ Your eyes sparkle

+ Ideas are always flowing

+ People around you feel drawn to interact

+ You have purpose and feel passionate about life

CONSIDER THIS YOUR GOAL FOR PERSONAL FREEDOM

EXPANDING

Becoming aware of your soul's guidance and following it expands your life experience.

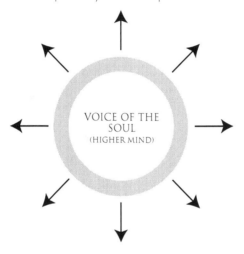

SHRINKING

Shrinking the dominance of your ego-mind liberates you from fear and the need to be in control.

+ Each day is a gift you appreciate

+ You are happy

+ Your heart is open

+ Your mind feels expanded

+ You give through kindness and caring

+ You find the beauty in all that is around you

+ You live in the moment

This is all possible when you let the inner wisdom of your soul guide you. In the next few chapters I will share ways to move from the dominating world of the VOE into the refreshing world of the VOS.

If you want to know whether the higher voice is talking to you, simply pay attention to how you feel. If you are feeling uplifted, inspired, energized, open in your heart, excited by ideas, passionate and peaceful, then you are aligned with the voice of your soul.

The VOS is always in the present moment. It is not a voice from the past or a voice that worries about the future. In the now the voice guides from a place of support and encouragement and invites you to be more of what you want to be. The *Voice of the Soul* is a true ally for creating a wonderful life in the present.

CHAPTER TWO

Why Following The Voice of the Soul Will Enrich Your Life

In the world there are many things going on that generate feelings of uncertainty and fear. The ego-mind is driven to protect us but it is really more like an overprotective parent who stifles his or her child despite the best of intentions. Over-parenting suppresses the individual expression and usually creates a lack of self-confidence in a child. The *Voice of the Ego* does very similar things to you and your life.

The *Voice of the Soul* is about personal liberation, self-realization and you being as fully you as possible. Yes, there are things out in the world to be careful of, but the soul is no easy fool. The VOS is also a great protector, *not because it generates fear but because it encourages awareness and being alert and fully awake in the world.* The VOS in the form of your intuition is always tuned in and will alert you to what you need to be aware of. This moment-to-moment awareness helps you make decisions that are not just about being safe but also about how you can be more open to what the present is offering you. In the now is where all the action is. The VOS lives in the moment and guides you to be available to the infinite potential and possibilities in the now.

Look around and remind yourself there is a much greater story than what appears on the surface. That story begins inside of you—where your spirit, soul and Higher Self are waiting to be explored. There is much more to your story than any dramas of life, than any personality tendencies, than any limiting beliefs that you think define you. You are part of a greater story of possibilities that resides in what is infinite and eternal in you. The VOS is your entryway into this world. The soul wants to share so much of what you are really made of and encourages you to explore and express your unique genius and greatness. Subscribe to any lesser story and you're selling yourself short.

You will begin to grow into a bigger story of who you are and what is possible when the VOS is the presiding influence.

The following is a list of the many benefits of the VOS being the guiding force in your life:

+   You will feel more alive and energized

+   You will become more self-realized as a human being

+   You will find it easier to choose happiness

+ You will explore and express more of your human potential

+ You will learn to liberate yourself from any self-limits and limiting beliefs

+ You will have more fun and be more creative

+ You will have more love in your life

+ You will express more of the endless capacity of your heart to love

+ You will open to the wisdom and insight within you

+ You will connect with the collective consciousness of humanity

+ You will be filled with appreciation for all life has to offer

+ You will have a clear sense of purpose

+ You will feel hope

+ You will find great passion for life

+ You will enjoy the many benefits of an open mind

+ You will find your way to inner peace

+ You will open to your connection with all beings

+ You will have greater clarity about ways to be successful

+ You will bring greater light into the world

+ You will be a joy for others to know

+ You will be more accepting of others

+ You will be empowered by the wisdom of your mind and heart

+ You will be more confident in all your expressions

+ You will be supportive and encouraging of others

+ You will create within yourself the best of health and well-being

+ You will learn to do life more effortlessly

+ You will see the world optimistically

+ You will be more interested in all of life

+ You will see the beauty that is all around you

+ You will feel balanced and harmonious

+ You will learn to live each day in the here and now, and view life as a wonderful celebration

A wonderful list, isn't it? Can you imagine all this is possible within you? If the answer is *yes*, then where do you go to be guided? That's right: you go to the Soul, your spirit, your Higher Self, which speaks to you through the *Voice of the Soul*.

If you can't imagine these possibilities in you, then the *voice of the ego* is running your life.

It is important to note that judging yourself in any way as not okay is the working of the VOE. You may hear the tone of self-judgment as you explore this book. Be mindful of those thoughts so you can label them as the VOE. In the process of labeling the VOE you take its power away and you bring yourself into the now, where the VOS resides.

Back to the bigger story. David Whyte, a poet, mystic and philosopher, says there is an essential conversation in each of us that allows us to find out who we are and what we need to do to more fully realize who we want to become. (See David if he is ever in your city because his words have the magic of touching your soul.) This inner conversation is about you, your soul and what is excitedly waiting in you to be expressed. Yes, excitement is the right idea here because beyond the confines of your ordinary mind is the unlimited you.

Let's speculate as to what a greater story might be like for you. Imagine if you fully step into the power within you. Imagine how that personal power would give you the courage to make a real difference in the world. That difference may be writing songs that uplift, or taking a leadership role in an organization working for the environment, it may turn you into a poet for peace, or drive you back to school to become a teacher who inspires others, or cause you to enter a training program on mindfulness so you can bring those practices to the world. Or you could become an advocate for those who are homeless, or a business leader who cares about the lives of your employees, or any other expression you could imagine.

Not long ago I was listening to an interview with a young person who had gone from living a life centered around partying in New York City to becoming a world-traveling yoga teacher and advocate for those living with AIDS. Her energy was booming out of my car speakers and I thought, How did she become this bright light in the world? She became that bright light because she listened inwardly to the guidance made available to her from her soul.

That kind of personal transformation is

waiting in you ...

IT IS WHISPERING AT YOU RIGHT THIS MOMENT.

The soul is calling you to be empowered, to be a light that brightens the world. Can you hear the quiet guiding wisdom inside?

The list earlier in this chapter is a long one so I want to give you some simple clear indicators of when you have shifted from the VOE to the VOS.

Here are *ten key indicators* that your ego has been placed in the back seat and the soul is running the show:

+ Your body feels energized and fully alive

+ Your mind has a focused clarity

+ Your intuition is loud and clear

+ Your eyes sparkle and your light draws people to you

+ You feel relaxed, balanced and harmonious

+ You feel present, awake, alert and aware

+ You are positive, inspired and hopeful

+ You sense the unity of all beings

+ You feel passionate with purpose

+ Your heart is full of compassion

If you experience at least several of these indicators, there is a good chance that you are enjoying the guidance of your soul.

CHAPTER THREE

Shrinking the Voice of the Ego

As you have seen, the *Voice of the Ego* is a strong and influential force in your life. Understanding the ego's influence allows you to alter the role it plays in directing your life.

The ego is a human idea used to describe an inner protective force in all of us. If you are engaged in awareness you most likely have met your ego on a number of occasions. This voice wants to be right and in control. The ego-mind is the part of you that wants to protect you from what it imagines to be a fearful world. This world, from the voice of the ego's perspective, is one of survival of the fittest. The ego wants to be the strongest and the most powerful protector and commander of all the factors of life that can possibly be controlled.

When the VOE keeps you safe it is a gift. But when it confines you to narrowness and the seeking of power over everything, it creates great suffering. The ego says, "Let's make sure you are safe," by keeping your heart protected, by being sure you are right and looking good, by judging all who question you and see the world differently and by all the other endless rationalizations driven by a fearful mind.

Your protected heart is unable to fully love even those who matter most to you. This is a heavy cost to pay. Without access to your heart, compassion, caring and kindness seem mostly out of reach. It is a cold world if the ego is master.

If being right matters more to you than your own truth, then welcome to Ego-land—where right makes might. In this land you depend only on yourself because everyone else is less capable than you. Being King of the Hill is what drives this win-or-lose frame of mind.

Imagine how your life would be if what others thought of you was all that really mattered. For the ego, what others think of you is a driving force. The ego needs the approval. Its survival is dependent on being accepted. If your sense of self is shaped by opinions of others, how do you feel? Probably not so good.

What about all those "crazy" people who don't agree with you? The ego needs to judge everyone as good or bad, for you or against you, in your camp or in the enemy camp. There is no room for growth, insight or awakening if nothing is right except what you think. What happens if your thinking is wrong? It is. If you don't question your thoughts, your beliefs are channeling your mind even more deeply into falsehoods.

The way of the VOE is full of peril, yet it dominates the world. This perilous voice tries to run our show. But the question is: can this kind of world be sustainably built on the slippery sands of power-seeking determination? The answer is no. Those who see themselves as in charge will give all they've got to come out as winners. Sadly, it is a game no one can win. Even if you hold on for a lifetime, death will have the upper hand and you will not have known peace in your heart.

The time has come to look at the picture of what the VOE has created by the very best of its collective ego-mind. There have been nonstop wars where lives are lost and people are forever damaged. Many religious and political extremists, in their sureness of being right, have led people into these wars to prove their superiority. The planet is being compromised by the call for endless growth run by the ego's need to have more. Many go hungry and are left homeless while others live in endless rationalized wealth. Our healthcare system can cause a middle-class family to lose everything, but such "unfortunate" circumstances are rationalized through profits and power. Financial institutions were "bailed out" because they were Too Big to Fail, according to those who rationalize greed. Schools lack innovation and push out creativity in favor of test scores and winning football teams. The world of entertainment and professional sports distracts us from what is not working and from our own discontent. All of this represents the work of the ego-in-charge.

There is also a more pernicious aspect of the VOE that

many are not aware of. It jails us in the past—into the old ways that haven't worked. It keeps harping on what could be if we only did it the way it should be done. It also puts us in the prison of worrying about the future. The ego is determined to control what's coming. It isn't in the present where real power exists.

This old story is leaking all over the place. The *Voice of the Ego* shouts loudly to plug the dam with old, faltering beliefs, but the cracks run too deep, and they continue to spread. There are no winners when systems fail and collapse—but the ego will rationalize it anyway. The story of blame is a great fallback story. You can blame others for not doing as you told them to do or for not following the "right way" as you prescribe it, when in reality this "right way" was the orchestrator of its own downfall.

Hanging on to blame is living on the precipice of
IGNORANCE AND BLIND WILL.

You can't go back no matter how much you try to have things as you imagined them to be. The past was not as ideal as you ego-mind likes to say it was. The VOE says, "Remember how it was? We can get back there again." You can try, but even a near brush with the best of the past will leave you empty in the now.

HOW TO SHRINK THIS VOICE

VOICE OF
THE EGO
(ORDINARY
MIND)

Self awareness

Observing your internal dialogue

Being mindful of your thoughts

Being present

Observing the fear and stepping beyond it

Opening your heart and loving

Turning the volume down on the inner critic

What Shrinks The *Voice of the Ego?*

First, this voice must be recognized for what it is. The recognition is not too difficult because it usually has fear and blame as its calling card. Once you are aware of that voice you can choose to ignore it and go in search of the higher wisdom of the VOS. **Awareness is the key.** The more aware you are of you inner dialogue and thoughts, the more you can choose to quiet the *Voice of the Ego.*

Shrink the VOE by refusing to feed it. You reinforce it when you choose to walk down the path of fear and blame— acting as if it is real. If you find yourself blaming others, situations, government, political parties or whatever, that means you feel powerless to do anything. The VOE hates to feel powerless but puts itself in the position regularly by blaming.

When you feel fear, acknowledge it. Then be courageous and do what your fear tells you not to do anyway. (Obviously, you should avoid doing things that are too dangerous, but remember that taking risks requires going against your fears.)

You can also shrink the *Voice of the Ego* by **living as fully in the now** as you can. The VOE has no power in the now. In the now, hope, happiness, freedom, love and peace of mind are what are present. It is only when you move into the future or back into the past with your mind that life seems scary and dangerous. In the now, everything is possible.

CHAPTER FOUR

Growing the
Voice of the Soul

There is a lightness of being that settles over you when the soul is running your life. This is because you are free to focus on what matters instead of hiding from what you fear and avoiding what you feel powerless to change. The Soul knows no boundaries, so the VOS can imagine endless possibilities for you and guide you toward the best of outcomes. This voice inside of you and me is all about seeking clarity, finding truth, being more conscious and living life with the freedom to fully express the possibilities within.

There are many methods and practices that will enrich your connection to the *Voice of the Soul*. I have experience with a number of those methods but I want to focus on three areas in which these practices can be categorized. These areas of exploration and awareness can help you find your way to your soul's wisdom and perspective.

HOW TO EXPAND THIS VOICE

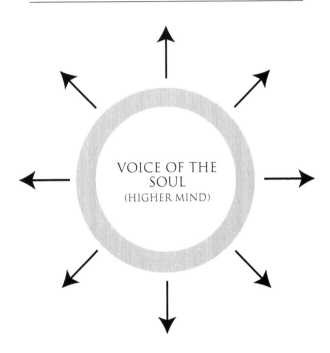

VOICE OF THE
SOUL
(HIGHER MIND)

Self love • Meditation

Quiet contemplation • Looking inward

Self awareness • Intuition

Impartiality • Mindfulness

Listening inward

Raising consciousness

Being present to mind, body & feeling

Expanding into your higher nature

The first path: Into The Silence

Into the silence means this exploration is about leaving the busy, noisy life behind and seeking silence instead. Being quiet is the method. This is about non-doing except for finding ways to be still and undisturbed. There is no trying to make things happen; instead the goal is to be fully in the moment.

In the silence there is the space necessary to build a relationship with your soul. Sitting and listening inward is the essence of this first path of exploration. It can be done in the silence of your home, in a quiet church, sitting in your car, out in nature and even, of all places, waiting in line where you may have lots of time to listen inward past the impatience and unrest of the mind.

The VOS may come in the form of intuition, messages from your heart, gut instincts or just a voice of knowing. When you listen, you'll discover there is great wisdom available—if you just take the time to tune inward.

A practice for the first path:

This exercise is very simple. Each day set aside time to be quiet. It could be early in the morning, late in the evening or taking a break during your day. Quiet time means no distractions—turn off the computer, the television or the music. It is time to be with yourself in respect for the deep wisdom that resides in your soul. Sitting and listening with a journal in your hand can be a wonderful way to allow the soul's voice to interact with you. Write down what you receive.

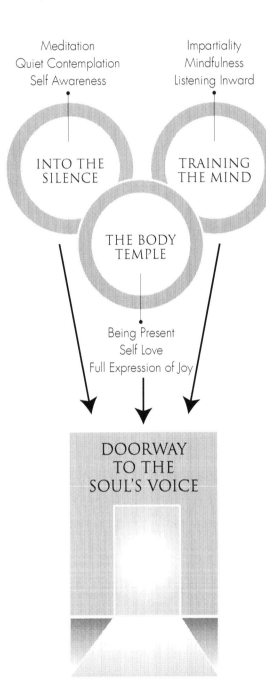

Meditation
Quiet Contemplation
Self Awareness

Impartiality
Mindfulness
Listening Inward

INTO THE
SILENCE

TRAINING
THE MIND

THE BODY
TEMPLE

Being Present
Self Love
Full Expression of Joy

DOORWAY
TO THE
SOUL'S VOICE

It has been my experience that if you go looking for silent spaces, they gladly present themselves throughout the day.

The second path: Training The Mind

This path is in pursuit of turning the mind into a more supportive friend that can help you find the doorway to your soul. There are many practices on this path including meditation and mindfulness, which are two of the most recognized forms.

Both meditation and mindfulness offer a variety of methods for encouraging the mind toward a deeper connection with your higher nature/soul. This path is the way of self-inquiry through the mind. It is also about expanding your self-awareness, bringing greater insight into your true nature and teaching you about what is going on inside in the form of thoughts and feelings.

Training the mind is also very beneficial for health and well-being. A well-trained mind is a clear path to the soul's infinite wisdom and a more expanded awareness and expression of who you are.

A practice for the second path:

If you take the time to notice your breath as it flows in and out, you become mindful. Following the breath is a wonderful, mindful practice. It brings you fully into the moment where the voice of the soul waits. You can be present to your breath anywhere. For example: waiting in line, driving a car or a golf ball, sitting at your desk, eating a meal, taking a shower and even, while working out. A watched breath slows you down and invites you to be aware. In awareness, the soul is always bringing light.

The third path: The Body Temple

This is the path of appreciating the body as a sacred vehicle on the soul's journey. Our physical connection to the soul is cultivated through practices that get us moving, dancing, stretching—pushing limits and being more alert and awake. Movement in many forms connects us to what is deeper and more expansive within us. In the West, dance and exercise have played a role in the body awakening to so much more. The influence of the East has brought us the vast potentials of yoga, tai chi and other body-centered practices.

On this path there are also less structured and disciplined ways. Two favorites for me are walks in nature and walking meditation. Taking a walk in nature is a direct connection to the infinity of creation. The whole body feels more alive when it communes with the forest, the desert, the ocean, the empty spaces and the rich vegetation, the vistas, the ripple of the creek, the warmth of the rock face, the stars on a dark clear night. All of this calls the soul out of the quiet depths.

In walking meditation, the body moves through space but transcends the doing. I discuss this practice in a novel I have recently been writing. In the story, I create an oval path through a forest in which my main character walks in a circle every day to bring light and inspiration to his life, to release what has gotten hung up in his emotional body and to expand his consciousness. At one point, he lifts off the ground because he and his soul have become free of any limits. I share this image because it resonates deeply within me—as if I shared that experience in my body as he did in his.

Another thing to understand about the body is that joy resides in your very cells. Joy is the soul in full expression, dancing in the moment and enjoying the gifts. When you feel most alive the soul is cheering you on with sweet support.

Other helpful methods include affirmations, visualization, contemplative prayer, chanting, centering practices and creative expression in many forms. Go exploring and find your own approach. The *Voice of the Soul* is here within, wanting to encourage and guide you—if you just ask. Your asking starts you on the way to becoming a positive force for good in the world. It's time. No more self-doubt. Let yourself be guided by the soul's voice and everyone on the planet will benefit from the expanded expression of who you are.

A practice for the third path:

This method brings your attention to your feet as you walk. It is called Foot Awareness. In this particular practice choose one foot. The foot that you intuitively sense can lead you directly to your soul. Feel this foot totally connected to the ground. Then begin walking—sensing this foot as you move. With practice you can be aware of your foot everywhere you go. Each time you tap into the foot and its contact with the earth, you open to the quiet knowing within. This even works, for example, when you're sitting in a less-than-interesting meeting. The minute you tune into the foot you become present—where the infinite possibilities of the now come alive as you open to the soul's guidance.

CHAPTER FIVE

The Benefits of the Voice of the Soul for the World

We live in a time that is rich with potential for great change. Communications through social media now bring us closer together and can create movements and even free whole nations from repressive regimes. The VOE and VOS both play important parts in what has been and what will be.

The VOE has dominated the world for centuries. The ego-mind is by its nature dominating. It wants control and it will do what it must to gain control. You can see the problems created by ego-driven-minds—governments that function poorly and powerful corporations that are driven by influence and profit. The ego-mind is not sustainable. It rationalizes insanity—wars that maim and kill and behavior that is destroying the planet. Future generations are not considered by the ego-mind because it only seeks control of the near future, where all it wants seems to be.

Of course much of the power-driven mind's best thinking is far from true. Fear- and power-seeking too often get in the way of the important questions. The mantra of the ego is "More, more, more" and questions about the impact of wanting are not entertained. Truth gets shaped into what serves the seeking of control. There is no bigger picture because the ego-shaped thinking is very narrow in its perspective.

A Broader Viewpoint

A much broader point of view is necessary for the good of the people and the planet. The *Voice of the Soul* has the ultimate in broad perspectives. It sees through all of time with an impartial objectivity, simply noting what is. There is the truth of what is seen, there are the questions of what can be learned, and there is the gathering together of the collective knowing of all souls. The VOS is the infinite wisdom of all souls and the highest knowing of the source of all souls— God, consciousness, the unknown, Buddha Mind, Great Spirit, Source Energy or whatever else you want to call it.

The source of all souls is an interesting thing to consider. Since neither you nor I are the creators of the universe, I believe it is safe to say there are creative forces greater than us. This force or source is the ultimate guidance for the soul's voice. The VOS can be seen and experienced as coming from the greatest wisdom of the Universe. This knowing exists beyond the boundaries of the ordinary mind, which is almost totally driven by the concerns, worries and fears of the ego-mind.

Let's you and I put our heads and hearts together and imagine what is possible:

Imagine a world that is free of worry, fear and judgment. A world free of the need to block the heart to feel safe, the need to be in control, the need to be right or the need to rationalize what we know is wrong.

Imagine a place where people gather together to work on solutions for the problems that are present within our communities.

Imagine a world where we act from the wisdom of our hearts with compassion, caring and loving-kindness towards all of our brothers and sisters.

Imagine a world where everyone is accepted for who they are and what their beliefs may be.

Imagine a world were there is no need for war because there are no enemies.

Imagine a world where there is no hunger or homelessness because collectively we have figured out how to take care of each other.

INTERFACING WITH THE WORLD

LIVE THIS:

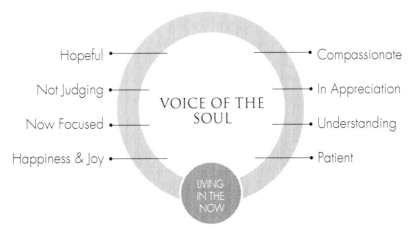

Hopeful •—————————————• Compassionate

Not Judging •—————————————• In Appreciation

VOICE OF THE SOUL

Now Focused •—————————————• Understanding

Happiness & Joy •—————————————• Patient

LIVING IN THE NOW

NOT THIS:

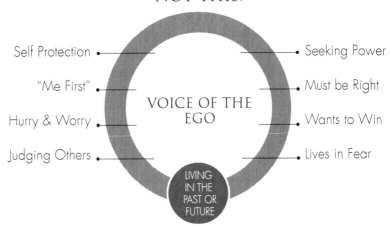

Self Protection •—————————————• Seeking Power

"Me First" •—————————————• Must be Right

VOICE OF THE EGO

Hurry & Worry •—————————————• Wants to Win

Judging Others •—————————————• Lives in Fear

LIVING IN THE PAST OR FUTURE

Imagine a world where there are no winners or losers—just fun competition.

Imagine a world where "the people" are the leaders guided by good sense, wisdom, collaboration and the foresight to care for the needs of future generations.

The heart and soul within all of us has a huge capacity to resolve all human concerns, to help everyone meet all their basic needs and to help us all encourage the best in each other. You don't have to live in doubt, scarcity, fear or wanting. You can instead live in hope and love, expressing yourself as fully as you desire and serving your fellow human beings. In doing so, you will leave the world better than what it would have been without you.

There are certainly grave issues all of humanity faces ahead, but with the *Voice of the Soul* guiding us there is a greater potential for bettering that which needs to be improved and for eliminating that which needs to be replaced.

Let your mind expand into what is possible if we all work together on the following pressing issues of the 21st century:

+ **Education is in need of great reform** to encourage people to realize their innate wisdom and greatness.

- **The earth needs to be better cared for** so everyone has clean air, water and soil now, and for future generations to live and love.

- **The political process needs to be repaired** so that the needs of the people are better represented.

- **Corporations need to be guided** to serve humanity instead of having "profits above all" be their guiding force.

- **All wars must cease** because to kill each other makes no sense to people who are guided by their souls.

- **Creativity is so essential** to the flowering of the human potential that it must become a core aspect of all our learning.

- **People who commit crimes must be helped** and offered treatment. They have been damaged by society and we must assist them in returning to health.

- **All hunger and homelessness will simply come to an end** when we use the vast resources of the planet for the good of all.

- **We must move from the haves and have-nots** to all needs being met. If we make better use of available resources and our own human wisdom, we can all live a fulfilled life.

- **We must end the extinction of other species.** We have gone off course and forgotten that all life is important. If other life forms are dying off in our world, it should be clear we must move toward more harmony and balance on the planet.

There will always be issues we need to work on together. These challenges will help us grow for the betterment of all living beings on the planet.

What matters to you? Let the *Voice of the Soul* guide you to be an effective agent of change. If the ego's voice is in charge, you may become too invested in doing it your way, being the boss, or going after what you want from the point of fear. Which voice will feel better and be the most effective?

The *Voice of the Soul* sits quietly waiting. Its kind and supportive guidance is there for you any time you need it. Are you ready to fully empower your life to serve humanity and the planet? What inner purpose calls you? What outer purpose encourages you into action in the world? If you have any questions, all you have to do is go inward, listen, and let yourself be guided. It is that simple if you befriend the *Voice of the Soul* and muffle the *Voice of the Ego*.

I hope you have a wonderful journey.

ABOUT THE AUTHOR

I have been counseling people for more than 35 years. During that time I've worked with people who were suicidal, had serious mental health issues and were drug addicts and alcoholics. I have debriefed many critical incidents such as bank robberies and workplace deaths. I have also taught other therapists and counselors how to be more effective. I have coached and consulted with individuals, athletes, small business owners and managers.

During my years as a helping professional, I've also focused on my own growth by participating in numerous workshops and furthering my education by earning my Masters Degree in Education in Counseling and my Doctorate in Counseling Psychology.

I was a competitive distance runner and played a number of sports. My explorations have taken me into yoga, tai chi and inner practices such as meditation, mindfulness and other methods for the expansion of higher consciousness. I have written a musical, three novels, two non-fiction books and a blog with more than 1700 posts. I have also explored abstract painting and collage.

As a social activist, I have focused on world peace by helping others find inner peace and by doing what I can to raise the collective consciousness and expand the compassion of the world. I am determined to leave the world a better place.

Human potential has always been one of my greatest interests and almost all that I have done is linked to my curiosity for what is possible in all of us. I enjoy inviting the potential out in everyone I meet.

I write all of this not to make me look like somebody extra special but to show my commitment to being as fully realized a human being as I can in this life and to invite that self-realization in as many other people as I can. Much of what I've done in this life has taught me more humility than self-importance, more courage than fear and to cultivate patience and acceptance instead of anger and critical judgment of others. The journey of my life has been so enriching and I am a better person because of it.

I hope my writings inspire the special in you to be realized.

Joseph Bernard

joseph@josephbernardpdh.com

www.explorelifeblog.com

Made in the USA
Charleston, SC
26 August 2013